Buffalo Memories III

THE EARLY YEARS AND THE 1950s

presented by

russell's
STEAKS · CHOPS · & MORE

ACKNOWLEDGMENTS

The Buffalo News is pleased to present *Buffalo Memories III: The Early Years and the 1950s*. It must be noted, however, that this unique pictorial history book would not have been possible without the generous contributions made by many people from virtually every corner of our community.
We are indebted, first of all, to those early area residents who captured their time—our history—in photographs, and provided a glimpse into their lives.
Secondly, all area residents are indebted to the many individuals who are committed to preserving our history in various libraries, historical societies, archives and personal collections throughout our community.

The following organizations have contributed greatly to this project:
The Buffalo & Erie County Public Library
The Buffalo History Museum

FOREWORD

Who can resist the 1950s?

Boys wore neckties to Catholic grammar school. Shops filled downtown storefronts. Women wore pencil skirts. Bathers packed Crystal Beach in mid-summer. WBEN-TV (BEN stood for Buffalo Evening News) featured local quiz shows and fashion demonstrations.

And in 1957, the Chef Felix Pizzeria on Wheels became the first food truck in Western New York.

This is the third edition of "Buffalo Memories," with more than 200 photos from Buffalo's early years through the 1950s. The 1950s was a great decade for Buffalo and Western New York. Lake freighters were still built in Buffalo. Ships lined the City Ship Canal in the wintertime, parked until Lake Erie became navigable again. At its Buffalo works, Worthington Corp. built engines that were two stories tall. And the Skyway debuted along the waterfront.

The 1950s brought its share of sorrow. Fires raged at St. John Kanty's Church, a General Mills storage bin and, tragically, at the German Roman Catholic Orphan Home and Cleveland Hill Elementary School.

It was also the decade that gave Buffalo police their first radar speed detectors.

Many of the photos in this book come from the archives of *The Buffalo News*. Others were generously made available by *News* readers, the Buffalo History Museum and the Buffalo & Erie County Public Library.

Bruce Andriatch, assistant managing editor for features, wrote the introductions to each chapter. Assistant Managing Editor Margaret Kenny edited the book and wrote the picture captions.

Enjoy these scenes from Buffalo's past.

Mike Connelly
Editor, *The Buffalo News*

TABLE OF CONTENTS

OPPOSITE: The Bank of Buffalo, then a branch of the Marine Trust Co., circa 1920s. The bank opened on Sept. 11, 1917, at the corner of North Division and Main streets. The building was torn down in 1964. JERRY M. MALLOY

CHAPTER ONE

THE EARLY YEARS

There's something about the turn of a century that seems to bring about rapid change. It was true of the technological revolution that presaged the 21st century and it was just as true in Buffalo 100 years earlier as people got accustomed to new and seemingly impossible forms of transportation, such as the motor car and the airplane. The changes would eventually herald the end of the city's golden era as a shipping mecca, but the city and its residents both were still growing and thriving when the calendar made its historic leap.

Between 1870 and 1910, as immigration into the United States from Europe accelerated, Buffalo's population nearly tripled, which is evident in photographs of large families and of crowded school classrooms.

The century started with the Pan-American Exposition, an event that was supposed to celebrate and cement the city's standing as a beacon for the world. It instead became a black mark with the assassination of President William McKinley, whose death here in 1901 led to a monument being erected in his honor before the end of the century's first decade that still stands in the shadow of City Hall.

It would be decades after McKinley's death that City Hall was completed, but Buffalo of the early 20th century already was home to buildings that still dot the downtown landscape today, including the Hotel Lafayette, the golden-domed Buffalo Savings Bank building, the Niagara Mohawk Building across the street, and the Old Post Office, which was the tallest building in Buffalo until 1912.

For recreation, Buffalonians did at least some of what Buffalonians of today still do: take a walk around the lake at Delaware Park or head to Canada to spend a day at Crystal Beach. But the changes that came with the flipping of a page on the calendar just kept coming.

OPPOSITE: Labor Day parade, Main Street, circa 1900. LIBRARY OF CONGRESS, PRINTS & PHOTOGRAPHS DIVISION, DETROIT PUBLISHING COMPANY COLLECTION, LC-DIG-DET-4A08405

ABOVE: Tillie Ernst's confirmation, circa 1889. RICHARD GIBSON

ABOVE RIGHT: Joseph A. Eger Jr.'s candy and cigar store at 426 Broadway in the late 1880s. Proprietor Joseph A. Eger Jr. is in the dark suit, and his son is to his left. ANN EGER THUMAN

RIGHT: The Gustavus Anderson family, late 1800s. DAISY ESTELLE ANDERSON

OPPOSITE: International Bridge, circa 1890. BUFFALO & ERIE COUNTY PUBLIC LIBRARY

ABOVE: William Street, circa 1895. Buffalo News Archives

LEFT: Engine Company No. 1 on South Division Street, late 1800s. Buffalo History Museum

OPPOSITE LEFT: Fred Hirsekorn and the former Clara Schottin on their wedding day, June 14, 1893. Nancy A. Fitzpatrick

OPPOSITE RIGHT: Louis and Matilda Roth on their wedding day in Buffalo in 1890. Marilyn J. Newman

ABOVE: The 31st National Encampment of the Grand Army of the Republic assembled in Buffalo in August 1897. The GAR was a fraternal organization composed of veterans of the Union forces during the Civil War, with a peak enrollment of 490,000 members in 1890. It held a "National Encampment" annually from 1866 to 1949. Josiah Wyatt Willis, great-grandfather of the photo donor, is 10th from left. DEBORAH WENDT

RIGHT: The eighth-grade class from School 32 in 1897 on Clinton Street. JAMES MAYER

OPPOSITE BOTTOM: Altman's Men's Store at 278 Main St., circa 1890. Standing at left in front of the store window is the photo donor's great-grandfather, John D. Fischer, who was a clerk at the store. JAMES MAYER

ABOVE: The family of James Anderson, at top, including from left, Emelia, Jerold and Olive, in the late 1800s.
DAISY ESTELLE ANDERSON

ABOVE LEFT: New York Central Railroad freight sheds, circa 1900. LIBRARY OF CONGRESS, PRINTS & PHOTOGRAPHS DIVISION, DETROIT PUBLISHING COMPANY COLLECTION, LC-D401-12923

LEFT: River and elevators, Main Street, circa 1900. LIBRARY OF CONGRESS, PRINTS & PHOTOGRAPHS DIVISION, DETROIT PUBLISHING COMPANY COLLECTION, LC-DIG-DET-4A07180

OPPOSITE: Unloading ore and loading fuel at the Lackawanna ore docks, circa 1900. LIBRARY OF CONGRESS, PRINTS & PHOTOGRAPHS DIVISION, DETROIT PUBLISHING COMPANY COLLECTION, LC-DIG-DET-4A08425

ABOVE: Lucy (Heibach) Schunk of 35 C St., circa 1901. MARCIA WOPPERER

ABOVE RIGHT: The children of John and Agnes Fischer in 1900. From left, Florence, Albert, Elma, Anna and Mildred. JAMES MAYER

RIGHT: The Pan-American Exposition in 1901, as seen from the corner of Elmwood and Amherst streets. JERRY M. MALLOY

OPPOSITE: Buffalo Savings Bank at 545 Main St., circa 1904. The building was designed by Buffalo architect E.B. Green and was completed in 1901. The building's iconic golden dome was added in 1953. LIBRARY OF CONGRESS, PRINTS & PHOTOGRAPHS DIVISION, DETROIT PUBLISHING COMPANY COLLECTION, LC-DIG-DET-4A12140

ABOVE: Pupils at St. Vincent de Paul School, circa 1905. The school was at Main Street and Eastwood Place. Joseph C. Voisard is in the front row, second from left. PAUL E. VOISARD

LEFT: The Post Office at 121 Ellicott St., circa 1905. When it opened in 1901, it had the distinction of being Buffalo's tallest building. LIBRARY OF CONGRESS, PRINTS & PHOTOGRAPHS DIVISION, DETROIT PUBLISHING COMPANY COLLECTION, LC-DIG-DET-4A12139

OPPOSITE: Looking up Main Street from the Erie Canal, circa 1905. LIBRARY OF CONGRESS, PRINTS & PHOTOGRAPHS DIVISION, DETROIT PUBLISHING COMPANY COLLECTION, LC-DIG-DET-4A12812

ABOVE: The Krupp family in front of their home on Sage Street in South Buffalo, circa 1907. The photo donor's grandmother, Bertha Krupp, is in the middle of the front row. BARB AND JOHN PARKINSON

RIGHT: Anthony Guercio, left, and his brother-in-law, Vincent Tremante, with their bicycles on Delaware Avenue, circa 1906. The two men were both tailors. Guercio eventually opened a shop at 322 Franklin St. ARTHUR J. PICOGNA

OPPOSITE LEFT: George and Josephine Fritton on their wedding day, June 5, 1907. MARY R. MANNING

OPPOSITE RIGHT: McCarthy siblings in 1907. THE SHAUGHNESSY FAMILY

ABOVE: Row boats on the lake in Delaware Park, circa 1908. LIBRARY OF CONGRESS, PRINTS & PHOTOGRAPHS DIVISION, DETROIT PUBLISHING COMPANY COLLECTION, LC-DIG-DET-4A22498

LEFT: Thornberger hoists being used to unload ore at the Lackawanna ore docks, circa 1910. LIBRARY OF CONGRESS, PRINTS & PHOTOGRAPHS DIVISION, DETROIT PUBLISHING COMPANY COLLECTION, LC-DIG-DET-4A08424

OPPOSITE: The Lafayette Hotel as seen from the center of Lafayette Square, circa 1908. The hotel, which was built in 1904, was designed by Louise Blanchard Bethune, the first known professional female architect in the United States. LIBRARY OF CONGRESS, PRINTS & PHOTOGRAPHS DIVISION, DETROIT PUBLISHING COMPANY COLLECTION, LC-DIG-DET-4A23150

ABOVE: A group of "Newsies" selling newspapers on Main Street in February 1910. LIBRARY OF CONGRESS, PRINTS & PHOTOGRAPHS DIVISION, LC-DIG-NCLC-03395

ABOVE RIGHT: The Drescher family, circa 1910. Albert Drescher is at far right, and his children are on the steps. Florence Drescher is the third girl on the right in the first row of girls. MELINDA VENTOLA

RIGHT: Early suffrage parade in Buffalo, circa 1910. ANN EGER THUMAN

OPPOSITE: The McKinley Monument in Niagara Square, circa 1910. LIBRARY OF CONGRESS, PRINTS & PHOTOGRAPHS DIVISION, DETROIT PUBLISHING COMPANY COLLECTION, LC-DIG-DET-4A25257

ABOVE: Main Street and Shelton Square, circa 1911. LIBRARY OF CONGRESS, PRINTS & PHOTOGRAPHS DIVISION, LC-DIG-DS-05281

LEFT: Watchman's office at the Pratt & Lambert Factory on Tonawanda Street, June 1911. Night watchman Charles Denver, left, is talking with the plant superintendent. CHARLES E. DENVER

OPPOSITE: Lafayette Square, circa 1912. LIBRARY OF CONGRESS, PRINTS & PHOTOGRAPHS DIVISION, DETROIT PUBLISHING COMPANY COLLECTION, LC-DIG-DET-4A25249

ABOVE: Graduating class of School 48 in 1912. Josiah Wyatt Willis, standing far right, was a teacher and principal in Buffalo schools for 50 years. DEBORAH WENDT

RIGHT: Charles A. and Minnie Ehlers with children Carlton Ehlers and Devillo Hoffman in front of the family's grocery store on Hamilton Street, circa 1912. Holding the horse at right is Robert Youngman. RICHARD EHLERS

OPPOSITE LEFT: The Electric Building at 20 East Huron St. on Oct. 23, 1912. LIBRARY OF CONGRESS, PRINTS & PHOTOGRAPHS DIVISION, LC-DIG-PPMSCA-41915

OPPOSITE RIGHT: John and Edward O'Malley, ages 5 and 3, on a mule in front of their home at 147 Potomac Ave. on Buffalo's West Side, circa 1912. CAROL VERDI

ABOVE: The steamer "Juniata" passing by the lighthouses at the entrance to the harbor, circa 1915. LIBRARY OF CONGRESS, PRINTS & PHOTOGRAPHS DIVISION, DETROIT PUBLISHING COMPANY COLLECTION, LC-DIG-DET-4A24366

LEFT: Classroom 22 in School 62 on Urban Street, circa 1913. EVELYN SWARTS

OPPOSITE LEFT: John A. Wessell, age 9, and George F. Wessell, age 7, circa 1915. SUSAN E. (WESSELL) WALKER

OPPOSITE RIGHT: Mary Kotrys shortly after she arrived in the United States from Poland, circa 1914. JENNIFER ARMSTRONG

ABOVE: The Napoleon Hotel at 101 Main St. in 1917. The hotel offered a free lunch, which was a big attraction at the time. Proprietor Godfrey Preneveau is behind the counter, second from left. MARY KELLER

RIGHT: Joe Kahen on the beach at Crystal Beach, Ont., just before leaving for World War I. NANCY YAEGER

OPPOSITE: C.R. Hea and his crew on the front of a Delaware, Lackawanna & Western Railroad (DL&W) locomotive on Sept. 8, 1916. LAWRENCE BRENTON

ABOVE: Godfrey Prenevall and his family out for a Sunday drive in this Willys-Overland (the name that meant Jeep for decades), in 1917. Prenevall is in the center wearing white cap; he is with his sons, Bill and Joe, and his daughter, Beatrice. MARY KELLER

LEFT: Mary Ellen (McCarthy) Shaughnessy in her First Communion dress, 1917. THE SHAUGHNESSY FAMILY

OPPOSITE: Buffalo Supply Committee, a group of men who help in the Red Cross Canteen in Buffalo, circa 1918. Many of the men were retired Army Officers. LIBRARY OF CONGRESS, AMERICAN NATIONAL RED CROSS PHOTOGRAPH COLLECTION, LC-DIG-ANRC-07037

ABOVE: Three generations of the Schick family at 109 Kingsley St. in 1918 are Christine Kumpf Schick, left, her daughter Edna Schick Glass, right, and Edna's son Eugene. SUSAN STYLES

LEFT: Hoctor's Grocery Store, 198 Masten Ave., circa 1918. From left: Huck, unidentified, and Martin R. Hoctor. WILLIAM M. HOCTOR

OPPOSITE: Nineteen-year-old aviator Katherine Stinson preparing for her flight from Buffalo to Washington, D.C., in connection with American Red Cross week in July 1918. Flying in her JN-4D 'Jenny' biplane, Stinson picked up the contributions to the Red Cross totaling $100,000,000 at Buffalo, Rochester, Syracuse, Albany, New York, Philadelphia and Baltimore. She then carried the checks to Treasury Secretary William G. McAdoo, who received her personally on the steps of the United States Treasury in Washington. LIBRARY OF CONGRESS, AMERICAN NATIONAL RED CROSS PHOTOGRAPH COLLECTION, LC-DIG-ANRC-08528

ABOVE: A delivery truck hauling King sewing machines, circa 1918. COLLECTION OF JASON CORYER

OPPOSITE TOP LEFT: Frances Pfeiffer near the ticket booth at Crystal Beach amusement part in Ontario in 1919. BETTY PFEIFFER

OPPOSITE BOTTOM LEFT: The Karas siblings, Henry, Sophia and Chester, circa 1919. CATHERINE KOLODZIEJ ERRINGTON

OPPOSITE RIGHT: The wedding photo of the former Frances M. Deuinger and George Pfeiffer in October 1919. Others in the photo are Harold and Louise Lang. JUDY ANN DIETRICH TODARO

FISH MARKET
BROWNROUTS
FRESH BONELESS FISH
OYSTERS
OYSTERS
BROWNROUT'S
BROWNROUT'S
FISH MARKET
1052 ELMWOOD AVE. AT BIRD AVE.
LI. 1460
WHITE FISH
YELLOW PIKE

HEATED APARTMENT
FOR RENT
575 BIRD AVE.

CHAPTER TWO

THE 1920s AND 1930s

The era between the two World Wars is also known by its polar opposite decades: one of great prosperity (The Roaring '20s) followed by one of unmatched economic catastrophe (The Great Depression). It also was the time period when women won the right to vote, when prohibition was passed and then repealed, and when the New Deal created a social safety net. Turmoil became a way of life.

Buffalo, which continued to swell in population to near its historic peak, was affected by all of it. But in photographs, its residents appear unfazed and unaffected. They went to work in small neighborhood businesses or monstrous manufacturing facilities; attended school; took part in civic clubs and activities; and always seemed to make time to be with their families.

As photography became more accessible to the masses, Buffalonians made sure to mark the important occasions in their lives, in photos of weddings, first communions and school graduations. When a family member had the security that came from a job, whether it was with the postal service, the fire department, or even as a carrier for *The Buffalo Evening News*, a photo recorded the person's pride.

A symbol of the connection with the country on the other side of the Niagara River became an everyday part of life as work crews began and then completed work on the Peace Bridge, connecting Buffalo and Fort Erie. The first of tens of millions of vehicles to make the familiar trip into Canada did so in 1927.

Another iconic structure came to life during this period, as workers in 1929 began construction on what would become the Art Deco masterpiece City Hall. The building opened for business with an official dedication less than three years later. In 1999, it was listed on the National Register of Historic Places.

OPPOSITE: The first storefront location of Brownrout Fish Market shortly after it opened at 1052 Elmwood Ave. at the corner of Bird Avenue, 1931. Standing, from left: Al Brownrout, his brother Louis and employee Dave Jenchil. Brownrout Seafood originated in 1928 when the brothers began operations in the back of Hoffman's Meat Market at 934 Elmwood Ave. In 1942, they moved their business to its final location at 451 Elmwood Ave. and remained there until 1983 when the business was sold to Schneider Fish & Seafood Company. In the 1960s, Brownrout Seafood was reported to have been the largest seafood distributor outside of coastal port areas. GERALD I. BROWNROUT

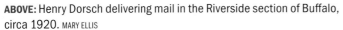

ABOVE: Henry Dorsch delivering mail in the Riverside section of Buffalo, circa 1920. MARY ELLIS

ABOVE RIGHT: Orchestra in the 1920s featuring Giuseppe "Joseph" Masino on harp, far left. SYDNE MASINO

RIGHT: Lalia Paschke sits sidesaddle on an Indian motorcycle with Ray Paschke Sr. standing next to her, circa 1920. LILLIAN MILLIMAN

OPPOSITE: Blessed Trinity School class photo, 1921. Howard Neubecker is fifth from left, standing in front of the chalkboard. JAY NEUBECKER

ABOVE: Eighth-graders in front of School 60, the former Riverside Academy, in 1923. George Wessell, uncle of the donor, is in the back row on the right, the tallest boy wearing a white shirt and dark tie. He attended Harvard, Holy Cross and Canisius, wanting to be a lawyer. But he loved science, so he decided to become a teacher and taught for 48 years. SUSAN WALKER

OPPOSITE LEFT: George and Rose Keck attending a Halloween party in 1923. CAROL PYTEL

OPPOSITE RIGHT: The former Helen V. Radecki in her wedding dress on June 7, 1922. Helen saw a wedding dress she loved, but could not afford, in the window of a Broadway store. But she was an amazing designer and seamstress, so she made several trips to the store window and was able to copy the dress for her wedding to Walter Matuszewski. DANIELLE H. MAICHLE

ABOVE: Second annual picnic for employees of Pillsbury Flour Mills on Aug. 22, 1925. CAROL SCHMIDT

RIGHT: Louis Turri beside Turri Grinding Service truck on Stevens Avenue, 1939. Turri would take his truck to various merchants and butchers and sharpen knives on site in his truck. THE TURRI FAMILY

OPPOSITE TOP: A store owned by Jacob Franz and Elizabeth Franz located at 1333 Genesee St., circa 1925. THOMAS KROMER

OPPOSITE BOTTOM LEFT: Anthony Lombardo in his shoe shop at 78 School St., circa 1925. DR. THOMAS A. LOMBARDO JR.

OPPOSITE BOTTOM RIGHT: John Cheman (behind the wheel) with his family in South Buffalo, circa 1925. John's wife, Julia, is in the back seat. Also pictured are their sons Gus, Steve, John and Joe. BRIAN CHEMAN

ABOVE: The Peace Bridge under construction, in October 1926. BUFFALO NEWS ARCHIVES

LEFT: Woodlawn Beach, circa 1925. Squatting in center with four sturgeon are Walter Decker and his sister, Blanch. KEVIN SCHAUGER

OPPOSITE: The Lafayette High School Spanish Club in 1926. John Wessell is in the back row, second from left. SUSAN E. (WESSELL) WALKER

ABOVE: John Schaller, an original employee of the Peace Bridge, in his work uniform, circa 1927. JAMES SCHALLER

ABOVE RIGHT: Herbert Rung, back of carriage, on an outing in the city in 1927. THE TURRI FAMILY

RIGHT: Sisters Ryba and Clara Kiedrowska in front of a beauty parlor at 34 Reed St., circa 1927. ADELE HAAS

OPPOSITE: Seventh-grade classroom, Riverside Academy, 1919. John A. Wessell, on the right, in the back. John was taken out of school to help his father work for a few years. He returned and graduated from Lafayette School in 1926. SUSAN WALKER

ABOVE: The future site of Buffalo City Hall at 65 Niagara Square at the beginning of construction on Sept. 16, 1929. LIBRARY OF CONGRESS, PRINTS & PHOTOGRAPHS DIVISION, HABS NY,15-BUF,13--3

LEFT: William Braun, left, in his dry-cleaning and tailor shop at 229 Franklin St., circa 1927. KEVIN SCHAUGER

OPPOSITE LEFT: The wedding of Casmira Keidrowska to Vincent Ryba in 1928. ADELE HAAS

OPPOSITE RIGHT: Patricia and Virginia Zydowicz in 1928. RONALD E. ZYDOWICZ

ABOVE: The 1929 American Legion Junior Baseball Champions, known as the Burke Brothers of South Buffalo from Post 721. The trophy is located at South Buffalo Post 721 on Cazenovia Street. Front row, from left: Frank Cannon; Bern Brady; unidentified; Ray Burke, sponsor; Joe McCarthy, manager, New York Yankees; Jim Cotter; Bob Stedler, sports editor, the Buffalo Evening News. Back row: Ray Scharmach, Jimmy Crotty, Walter Kroczynski, Joe Donahue, Bill Joyce, Bob Downey, Cy O'Connell, Joe Smith, Don Jacobi, Father Flynn, Fran Russert, Jack Ford. THE JACOBI FAMILY

ABOVE RIGHT: Franz, Hoerner and Schmitz family picnic, circa 1929. BARBARA J. MURRAY

RIGHT: Amelia Earhart, third from left, at the Buffalo airport in March 1929. BUFFALO NEWS ARCHIVES

OPPOSITE: Consolidated Aircraft workers, late 1920s. At one time Lawrence "Larry" Bell, founder of Bell Aircraft, worked for Consolidated Aircraft. Bell launched his aviation career in the early 1900s with the Glenn Martin Company of Los Angeles. THE JACOBI FAMILY

ABOVE: The Società Serradifalco flag christening ceremony on Busti Avenue on June 8, 1930. The group is made up of immigrants from the same town in Sicily. DAVID GRISANTI

LEFT: Buffalo Police Commissioner Austin J. Roche, second from left, and Arthur D. Britt, right, then an auto squad lieutenant and later longtime Erie County Sheriff. They are showing off newly acquired guns that fire gas shells and illuminating star shells with parachutes. BUFFALO NEWS ARCHIVES

OPPOSITE: Erie County Savings Bank, 16 Niagara St., circa 1930. LIBRARY OF CONGRESS PRINTS AND PHOTOGRAPHS DIVISION, HABS NY,15-BUF,3--10

ABOVE: In his youth, Joseph Cardina sold *The Buffalo Evening News* in the Parkside neighborhood and later worked for *The News*, retiring as promotions manager in 1983. CAROL SCHMIDT

ABOVE RIGHT: Rear view of the Ford plant at 2495 Main St., 1930. Later, this building was known as Tri-Main Center, home to more than 100 companies. ROBERT KAISER

RIGHT: Brothers Bill and Herman Brauch, along with two of their friends, celebrate becoming U.S. citizens in 1932. WILLIAM J. BRAUCH

OPPOSITE: The Gaelic football team, champions of Western New York, circa 1931. Front row, from left: J. Flood, J. Brazil, P. Flanagan, J. Finn, M. Kelly, D. Scully. Middle row: D. Moynihan, M. O'Connor, E. Coughlin, G. Callahan, J. Coughlin. Back row: M. O'Connor, A. O'Dea, T. Doherty, J. Fitzgerald, M. McGarth. MARY MCGRATH KLIER

ABOVE: Graduating class of St. John Kanty School in June 1932. JOHN A. NOWAK

OPPOSITE TOP LEFT: Francis Xavier Peters, a captain with the Buffalo Fire Department in the 1930s. RUTH AUER

OPPOSITE BOTTOM LEFT: Students at the School of Beauty Culture at 320 Franklin St., circa 1932. Margaret Picogna is in the front row, third from left. ARTHUR J. PICOGNA

OPPOSITE RIGHT: Sylvia Galas Przybyl on her wedding day at Transfiguration Catholic Church in 1932. VICTORIA PRZYBYL LUCHOWSKI

ABOVE: Members of the Ghianni family in the driveway at 87 Interpark, circa 1933. Behind the wheel is Buona Ghianni. In front of the car, from left: Amedio Ghianni, Joe Ghianni, Nicole Vece. MARIE TIBURZI BENNY

ABOVE RIGHT: Joel Ziolo's first barber shop, northeast corner of Transit Road and Terrace Boulevard, circa 1934. ROBERT KAISER

RIGHT: Family of Mr. and Mrs. Anthony Lombardo, circa 1932. Seated, from left: Marion Lombardo, Anthony Lombardo, Mildred Lombardo. Standing: Thomas A. Lombardo Sr., Josephine Lombardo, Anthony Lombardo Sr., Philip Lombardo. Thomas A. Lombardo Sr. became a prominent pediatrician. DR. THOMAS A. LOMBARDO JR.

OPPOSITE: First Communion at St. Francis DeSales Church in 1932. SANDRA EICHELBERGER

ABOVE: John J. Thiell's First Communion at St. Gabriel's on Clinton Street in Elma, circa 1934. LORI MOLIK

ABOVE LEFT: St. Adalbert's School eighth-grade class in 1935. Valerie Janusz is seated in the front row, middle desk. DIANE TARDIBUONO

LEFT: Sturm's Harmony Orchestra playing at Chudy's, a dance hall on Genesee Street in the 1930s. Charles F. Schoy played trumpet, third from left, and J. Sturm played piano. GERARD KAWCZYNSKI

OPPOSITE: Confirmation class at Christ German Evangelical Church, Clinton and Baitz streets in 1935. The minister is Rev. Carl Vogelmann. WILLIAM SCHEIDER

ABOVE: Walter and Patty Bird in their backyard at 423 Baynes Street in 1937. Walter was a Buffalo fireman. Patty became a detective and sergeant with the Sheriff's Department. PAT SIRACUSE

ABOVE RIGHT: Annual Republican "Capitol Hill Show," 1930s. One of the performers is Nathan Freedman, owner of Chippewa Loan and Jewelry. NANCY FREEDMAN SCHILLER

RIGHT: Helen Ladika with the family car on Condon Avenue, circa 1936. BRIAN CHEMAN

OPPOSITE: Casmira and Vincent Ryba with their children, Theresa, Adele and Vincent, in front of Ryba's Meat Market on Broadway, circa 1936. ADELE HAAS

ABOVE: Celina (Rung) Turri, third from left, and others enjoying a family gathering at the beach in Evans, circa 1937. THE TURRI FAMILY

OPPOSITE LEFT: Theodore and Elizabeth Martin play with their new toys on Christmas in 1937. BONNIE MARTIN

OPPOSITE RIGHT: Mr. and Mrs. Edward Liszka's wedding photo in 1937. RONALD WACHOWSKI

ABOVE: Edward Foisset, who was a mail carrier from June 1937 through October 1967, at his home at 83 Berwyn Ave. on July 18, 1937. JANET M. FOISSET

ABOVE RIGHT: Mary Lee Robinson (owner) and her two sons — Thomas, left, and Ulysses Jr. — displaying baked goods at Kozzy Bake Shop at 284 Jefferson Ave., circa 1938. The bakery specialized in pies, cakes, rolls, donuts and cookies. CHARLES H. CAMPBELL

RIGHT: Saglibene's grocery store at York and 14th streets, circa 1938. Salvatore Saglibene is at right and his sister-in-law, Sadie Giambra, is at left. DR. THOMAS A. LOMBARDO JR.

OPPOSITE: Ralph's Food Market on Walden Avenue in 1938. SHEILA AND JEFF CARREL

ABOVE: The five sons of Otto Wieand taking in the sun on the running board of their father's late 1930s Buick at 33 Olcott Place, Cheektowaga in 1939. Their father is seated inside the car on the passenger side. WALTER WIEAND

LEFT: James and Ora Anderson and their sons, Arthur and David, dressed up for a celebration, circa 1939. Ora was a Buffalo Club woman and a member of one of the oldest African American families in Buffalo. She was also Regional President of the Empire State Federation of Women's Clubs. DAISY ESTELLE ANDERSON

OPPOSITE: Railway Express sales conference at the Hotel Lafayette on March 28, 1939. DARWYN H. MEYERS

CHAPTER THREE

THE 1940s

The Unites States was an active participant in World War II for less than four years, but the war and its impact dominated every aspect of life in Buffalo for the entire decade.

One of the more conspicuous changes in the city was in the workplace, where factories were converted into armament and transportation manufacturers and women left their homes to do whatever job was needed to aid the war effort.

But the impact could be seen everywhere: in victory gardens in city backyards; in photos of young men about to be deployed and facing the prospect of never coming home; in long lines of people hoping to get gasoline for their vehicles or food for their families; in huge crowds turning out to see a Hollywood star in town to promote war bonds; and in parades meant to keep focus on the struggle to free the world.

Once the war ended and lives returned to something resembling normalcy, change could be seen almost anywhere. Perhaps there was no greater microcosm of that change than at the Bloedel Manufacturing Co. on East Ferry Street. During the war, it made aircraft parts. After the war, it made tricycles.

The post-war '40s brought prosperity to a growing middle class, but it didn't always come easy. It also was a time for the working class to assert itself in demands for better working conditions and wages or to organize with labor unions.

Changes in Buffalo came quickly in the post-war era as returning veterans and their families began looking beyond city boundaries for places to live. The city's population would near its peak by the decade's end, as the suburban migration began in earnest.

OPPOSITE: During World War II, women helped to solve the workforce shortage in the production of aircraft engines. This woman is removing excess stock with a burring tool from her work bench for assembly in Pratt & Whitney Aircraft Engines, circa 1943. The engines were produced in volume by Chevrolet for bombers and cargo planes. BUFFALO NEWS ARCHIVES

ABOVE: Thomas Clarence "Brownie" Brown with his new car on Matthew Street, circa 1940. Brown owned a number of gas stations and car mechanic businesses as well as bars, primarily in the William and Jefferson area and Cold Springs. CHARLES H. CAMPBELL

ABOVE RIGHT: Smith's Pharmacy soda fountain at Grant and Ferry streets in 1940. According to a sign on the wall, a pint of ice cream could be purchased for 30 cents. ALLAN SMITH

RIGHT: Rev. and Mrs. Nash along with Thelma Anderson, Sandra Anderson, James Anderson Jr. and Diane Anderson, recipients of the Jesse Ketchum medal, in the early 1940s. The Jesse Ketchum Awards celebrated academic excellence in the Buffalo Public Schools. Ketchum was a wealthy Buffalo businessman and philanthropist who gave to educational and religious causes. He was a founder of Westminster Presbyterian Church and the school that eventually became SUNY Buffalo State. Ketchum died in 1867 at age 85. DAISY ESTELLE ANDERSON

OPPOSITE: Construction work on grain silos, circa 1940. LOUISE CARR

ABOVE: Harry Reiser and his wife, Mary Kolb Reiser, working in the store and meat market they founded at Ontario and Evelyn streets in Riverside, circa 1940. Harry and Mary lived upstairs from the store with their children, Charles, Mary, Henry and Eddie; everyone spent time working in the store. CHARLES REISER JR.

ABOVE LEFT: Martin Slon tends bar at Slon's Tavern, 508 Peckham St., circa 1940. The bar was ideally located across from the Central Terminal during the heyday of trains. A trap door at the end of the bar led to a basement where homemade beer was stored during prohibition. N. JOHN FILIPOWICZ AND AMY FILIPOWICZ

LEFT: The Bird family at 423 Baynes St., circa 1940. From left: Rita, Bernard, Lillian, Patty, Walter, Lill. Bernard Bird was the Buffalo city treasurer in the late 1940s. PATRICIA SIRACUSE

OPPOSITE: Elizabeth "Lee" Peters Fingerle and Charles Fingerle in the backyard of their home on Winspear Road, circa 1940. RUTH AUER

RIGHT: The front of the newly completed Apollo Theater, April 1941. It was first opened as a movie theater by the Basil Brothers and for many years, the 900-seat theater provided hours of entertainment. It was a hub of activity on the Jefferson Avenue commercial strip. The theater stopped showing movies when a fire caused extensive damage in 1966. It was subsequently used for community gatherings and other various activities until it was abandoned in the late 1980s and taken over by the city in a tax foreclosure proceeding. In recent years, the Apollo was converted into a telecommunications facility to provide state-of-the-art facilities for public, educational and governmental access. BUFFALO NEWS ARCHIVES

OPPOSITE TOP LEFT: Bethlehem Steel Company employees cast their ballots to decide whether they were to be represented by the C.I.O. Steel Workers Organizing Committee for purposes of collective bargaining in May 1941. The election was conducted under NLRB auspices. BUFFALO NEWS ARCHIVES

OPPOSITE BOTTOM LEFT: June Kaiser and a friend in a classic convertible at Transit Road and Terrace Boulevard in July 1941. ROBERT KAISER

OPPOSITE RIGHT: Clara J. Donavan inspecting links made for .50-caliber machine guns at the Fedders Manufacturing Company plant in November 1941. BUFFALO NEWS ARCHIVES

ABOVE: Neighborhood kids in a photo taken by the Buffalo school superintendent in 1941. Jacqueline (Shea) Wopperer is in the center of the back row and her brother, Robert, is sitting at right in the wagon. MARCIA WOPPERER

LEFT: Motorists line up to receive supplemental gas rationing books at Bennet High School on Aug. 24, 1942. Gas rationing was common during World War II. BUFFALO NEWS ARCHIVES

OPPOSITE: Thousands of people crowd Lafayette Square to see film star Irene Dunne, who visited Buffalo to help sell War Bonds and Stamps in September 1942. BUFFALO NEWS ARCHIVES

ABOVE: Daniel Breister in 1942. CLAIRE HUGHES

ABOVE RIGHT: Easter High Mass in Corpus Christi Church in April 1943. LIBRARY OF CONGRESS, PRINTS & PHOTOGRAPHS DIVISION, LC-DIG-FSA-8D28445

RIGHT: Plane building crew at Curtiss-Wright plant on Elmwood Avenue during World War II. Bertha Henely is at far right in the second row. ARLENE KELLEY

OPPOSITE: Gerald Mocny, far left, was an aviation mechanic for the Navy during World War II. AUDREY RUBINO

ABOVE: During the war, price controls were implemented on many consumer goods. Families had to register for ration books, and additional ration points could be earned by turning in food waste. Mrs. Robert Bond of Hampshire Street collected four cents and two brown ration points for turning in a pound of rendered kitchen fat to Anthony Scime of Scime Brothers Grocery in December 1943. BUFFALO NEWS ARCHIVES

LEFT: Peter Grimm, age 10, waiting with his wagon outside Loblaw's grocery store for customers to ask him to deliver their groceries in May 1943. LIBRARY OF CONGRESS, PRINTS & PHOTOGRAPHS DIVISION, LC-DIG-FSA-8D29090

OPPOSITE: Majorettes heading the contingent of the Army & Navy Drum Corps during a bond parade in April 1943. All military branches of service in Western New York were represented in the parade that lasted more than two hours. On this particular day, it was Newspaper Day in the bond drive, and American freedom of the press was stressed. BUFFALO NEWS ARCHIVES

ABOVE: Francis Malachowski with her victory garden on the back shed roof of the White Front Restaurant, 262 Ohio St. in 1943. She owned the restaurant and the garden provided fresh food for the restaurant. JERRY M. MALLOY

ABOVE RIGHT: Employees of the Curtiss-Wright war plant in 1943. DAISY ESTELLE ANDERSON

RIGHT: Soccer team at Genesee Park (Brown's Park), 2090 Genesee Street in 1944. In the front row, second from left is Alfons Meier, father of the donor. JOANNE WIEAND

OPPOSITE: The captain of the steamer "Greater Buffalo" (standing right) welcomes passengers transported from the Hotel Buffalo at Swan and Washington streets, circa 1943. The Studebaker built Tallyho coach the passengers arrived in was the hotel's unique workaround and promotion used to observe war time rationing of gasoline and rubber tires. JAMES BARR

ABOVE: Charles J. Campbell with his wife, Stella Scott Campbell, before his deployment to the Philippines in August 1944. CHARLES H. CAMPBELL

ABOVE LEFT: Break time for ladies working at the Leroy Avenue H&A Manufacturing plant in 1944. The company made small parts for airplanes during World War II. E. Dori Wessell is in the front row at right. SUSAN E. (WESSELL) WALKER

LEFT: Four generations of the Campbell family in the summer of 1944. From left: Charles Jay Campbell, Charles Walter Campbell, Charles Howard Campbell, Charles Knox Campbell. CHARLES H. CAMPBELL

OPPOSITE: A device attached to the automobile of John E. Bock was used to study Buffalo street lighting in April 1944. At the wheel is Bock, a General Electric Company illuminating engineer who tells what a motorist sees or doesn't see as he drives on highways and streets. BUFFALO NEWS ARCHIVES

ABOVE: Theresa (Lodico) Pace and her daughter Marie (Pace) Waterrose, circa 1945. MARIE (PACE) WATERROSE

ABOVE RIGHT: Emergency workers clearing snow and ice to free tracks into Buffalo from the icy grip of one of the city's worst blizzards in December 1945. BUFFALO NEWS ARCHIVES

RIGHT: Tibor J. Panty displaying a box of flowers in front of his delivery vehicle in the 1940s. He and his wife, Margaret, had just opened their first shop at 744 Tonawanda St. ELAINE M. PANTY

OPPOSITE: George Eberle in his grocery store at Forest Avenue and Tremont Street, circa 1945. DIANE SAGER

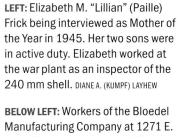

LEFT: Elizabeth M. "Lillian" (Paille) Frick being interviewed as Mother of the Year in 1945. Her two sons were in active duty. Elizabeth worked at the war plant as an inspector of the 240 mm shell. DIANE A. (KUMPF) LAYHEW

BELOW LEFT: Workers of the Bloedel Manufacturing Company at 1271 E. Ferry Street turned their skill from making aircraft parts during World War II to making tricycles after the war, June 1946. BUFFALO NEWS ARCHIVES

OPPOSITE: Marchers with signs wanting higher wages and lower food prices during a parade from Main to Niagara Square by way of Court Street in July 1946. BUFFALO NEWS ARCHIVES

ABOVE: Nick Tiburzi and Ange Ghianni at their wedding reception on Sept. 27, 1947. MARIE TIBURZI BENNY

ABOVE RIGHT: Mass at Civic Stadium, which was renamed War Memorial Stadium in 1960, during Eucharistic Congress on Sept. 24, 1947. BUFFALO NEWS ARCHIVES

RIGHT: Bernard and Helen Basinski join in a toast from their family members and friends at Nowakowski Tavern, Oct. 26, 1946. Located on Rother and Sycamore streets, Nowakowski Tavern was a well-known establishment owned by Bernard's grandparents. ELAINE SMITH

OPPOSITE: Even after the war ended, food shortages continued. This is the scene at the Mohican Market on Main Street near Fillmore in 1946, on a day when butter was available. Inside the market was a "mob scene," as Office of Price Administration rules dropped the price to 53 cents. Other markets, confused by the change in rules, were selling for 64 cents. The OPA was dissolved and price controls ended in 1947. BUFFALO NEWS ARCHIVES

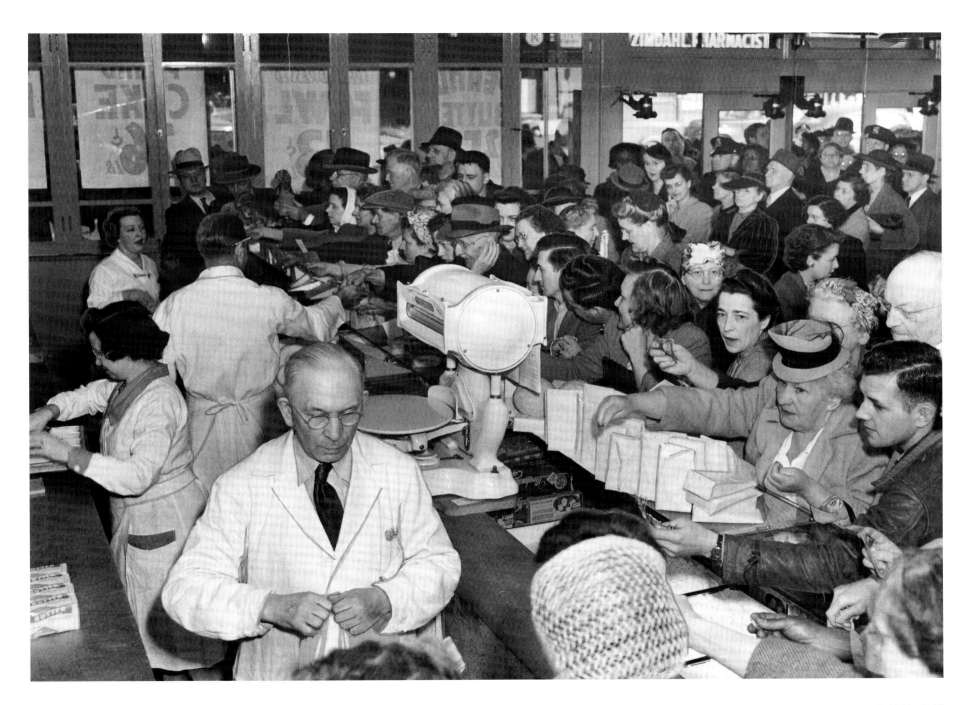

ABOVE: Lou Horwitz, president of Playboy Motor Car Corp., proudly shows off the 1947 Playboy at the Hotel Statler in February 1947. This was the premier showing of the new car built in Buffalo. The car featured a rear engine and was a soft-top convertible. DAVID KAPLAN

ABOVE LEFT: The Buffalo Police Department gets a centralized complaint setup in 1948. The heartbeat of the department's new system for dispatching and recording complaints is centralized at this table. Each of the six stations has two phones and lights replace bells. Desk lieutenants, clockwise, are Gregg F. Eberman, John C. Rapp, Royal E. Schrack, Glenn H. Bogardus, J. Stanley Bratt and Norman J. Koch. BUFFALO NEWS ARCHIVES

LEFT: Weekend dinner at Lorenzo's Restaurant, circa 1947. In the photo, at left, are Nora D. and Joseph J. Runfola and their daughter, Diane. At right are Nettie (Romanello) and Joseph Sperazz and their son, Johnny. DIANE E. RUNFOLA

OPPOSITE: The Buffalo River in October 1948. Once one of the world's most valuable industrial waterways, it slipped in rank due to it being too small to accommodate large lake freighters. BUFFALO NEWS ARCHIVES

RIGHT: Virginia Ballow, left, and Kathy Sullivan enjoying a snow day in front of Peter Blasius' shoe repair shop at 1280 E. Ferry St., circa 1948. EDWARD BALLOW

OPPOSITE TOP: Members of the Negro Registered Nurses of Buffalo when they presented their First Tea in 1948 at the Willert Park Center. From left: Mrs. Odessa Williams, Miss Grace Shallowhorn, Mrs. Placid Jean Parker, Mrs. Stella Campbell, Mrs. Eva Noles, Mrs. Elma Ellis, Mrs. Aviegale Lang, Miss Olive Benjamin, Mrs. Geneive Holmes, Mrs. Georgine Hairston, Mrs. Marjorie Robinson, Miss Frances Wofford, Miss Betty Barton, Mrs. Mamie Franks. Not present for the photo were Mrs. Alberta Fulton, Miss Camille Melton, Miss Thyra Merriweather. CHARLES H. CAMPBELL

OPPOSITE BOTTOM LEFT: Boy Scout Troop 102 at St. Lukes Church, Richmond and West Utica streets, circa 1948. Charley Lang (standing third from left) earned his Eagle Scout Award, served in the military during the Korean War and was scoutmaster of Troop 102 in the early 1960s. Front row, from left: Dick Cole, Tony Menza, Herb Boyce, unidentified, Jack Metz, Roger Draper, unidentified, Arnold Boyce. Back row: Russ Arnold, Ozzie Adle, Charley, Ken Taylor, Harley Highland, Ray Broster, Allen Merrifield, Ronnie Adle. JAMES BARR

OPPOSITE BOTTOM RIGHT: Lottie Wojciak behind the counter at her Tasty Cake Bake Shop, 59 Walden Ave., circa 1948. JANET ZUREK

ABOVE: Kindergartners in front of School 74 at Northland and Wohlers avenues, circa 1949. From left: Charles H. Campbell, Beckjane Robinson, Marilyn Victory. CHARLES H. CAMPBELL

ABOVE LEFT: A group of friends on Putnam Street ready for Easter Sunday, circa 1949. From left: Shirley Bird Britzzalaro, Melissa Warren, Dotty Young, Dee Harding. CATHY ALLMAN

LEFT: Buffalo Mayor Bernard J. Dowd shakes hands with Playboy Motor Car Corp. President Lou Horwitz at the opening of the company's new factory in the former Chevrolet Plant No. 1 on Kenmore Avenue in January 1948. Previous Playboy cars had been produced in a much smaller plant at 988 Ellicott St. DAVID KAPLAN

OPPOSITE: Playboy cars being hand built in the company's first factory at 988 Ellicott St., circa 1948. Lou Horwitz was the president of the company that built 97 cars in Buffalo from 1947 through 1949. DAVID KAPLAN

CHAPTER FOUR

THE 1950s

For Buffalo's first Baby Boomers, these were the good old days.

Jobs were plentiful. Downtown was thriving. Rock 'n' roll arrived – along with a fear that it was radicalizing teenagers.

But the real radical change came not from what was going on in the streets but what was coming into the city's living rooms: television sets.

The city's first television station WBEN-TV – the BEN stood for "Buffalo Evening News" because it was owned by the Butler family who owned the paper - had gone on the air in 1948 but gained popularity in the next decade as more people were able to buy sets. The station's call letter would later be changed to WIVB. Buffalo's two other over-the-air stations, WKBW and WGR – later WGRZ – both came to be in the 1950s.

The speed of technological innovation accelerated as the decade wore on in ways large and small. TV forever changed the way people were entertained, but other advances would affect people's lives. The police had a radar device that could tell if someone was speeding; hospitals could see the brain by way of X-ray; law enforcement could use a machine to transmit photographs between jurisdictions; and traffic lights could be synchronized for the increasingly mobile society to get where it needed to go.

No retelling of Buffalo in the 1950s would be complete without an understanding of how transportation decisions reshaped the region. Construction on the Kensington Expressway – commonly referred to as "the 33" – began in 1958 and made it easier for commuters to travel between the suburbs and the city. The elevated Skyway finished in 1955 would serve the same purpose for Southtowns commuters. Construction on the Niagara Section of the Thruway – the 190 – also began in the '50s.

Perhaps the most noteworthy thing to occur in the decade was something that had not happened in the city's history: a population decline. By the time 1960 dawned, the number of people living in Buffalo from 1950 had shrunk by nearly 50,000. It was a trend that has never been reversed.

OPPOSITE: Looking south on Main Street between Chippewa and Tupper in June 1950. BUFFALO NEWS ARCHIVES

ABOVE: Erwin Gluckman leads the house band at the Chez Ami, circa 1950. JOY SCIMÉ

ABOVE RIGHT: A typical scene at the WBEN-TV studios every Sunday evening at 6:30 pm, when Buffalo actors Kay Jones and Art Hunt enact the game of charades before cameras and competing teams, April 1950. Observing are Mrs. Gertrude R. Lorenz, Miss Marjorie M. Baker, Mrs. Lorraine Wilson Pankow, Nathaniel A. Barrell, Emcee Julian N. Trivers, Homer J. Savage and John H. Little. Mr. Barrell and Mrs. Pankow were permanent members of the panel. BUFFALO NEWS ARCHIVES

RIGHT: Reichlin Brothers auto repair, 3229 Bailey Ave., circa 1950. SHIRLEY TRINN (REICHLIN)

OPPOSITE: The Buffalo Police Department's new $5,645 prison van on display in 1950. The department sold the 1940 van for $1,081. At left is Patrolman Edward Forlich. Behind the wheel is Patrolman John C. Wienand. BUFFALO NEWS ARCHIVES

ABOVE: Neglected leaves clogged a receiver and led to a flood on Niagara Street and West Delavan Avenue in October 1950. BUFFALO NEWS ARCHIVES

LEFT: Shelton Square in July 1950. It was a crossroads for private cars and bus traffic. The thousands who traveled through it every day glanced at the traffic safety sign to see whether the city was running ahead or behind the traffic death totals of the prior year. BUFFALO NEWS ARCHIVES

OPPOSITE: Helicopters being produced at Bell Aircraft, December 1950. These helicopters were designed to handle five stretchers, or eight fully armed men or 10 unarmed men. BUFFALO NEWS ARCHIVES

ABOVE: Third- and fourth-grade students at St. Florian School at 567 Hertel Ave., circa 1950. The school closed in 1983, and the church closed in 2007. AUDREY KAMINSKI

RIGHT: Pelzer's Shoe Store at 1180 Lovejoy Street on Nov. 26, 1950. The store was established in 1922 by Charles and Bertha Pelzer. In 1945, their son, Art, and his wife, Ruth, became the new owners. The store closed in 1985. ROBERT AND CHERYL PARR

OPPOSITE LEFT: Mary Manning and her mother, Rose (Fritton) Manning in matching dresses made by Rose in 1950. MARY R. MANNING

OPPOSITE RIGHT: Patients at Millard Fillmore Hospital in the 1950s got music four times a day to help speed recovery. Nurse Ruth M. Long, right, checks with a patient before switching the music on, while nurse Rosalie M. Pingitore examines one of the long-playing records in the automatic player. BUFFALO NEWS ARCHIVES

ABOVE: The concession stand at the Buffalo Zoo in July 1951. BUFFALO NEWS ARCHIVES

LEFT: Five drivers in front of trucks owned by R. Black & Son's Trucking at the Clinton Street Market, circa 1950. The drivers are: Newton, Bley, Bates, Hassell, unidentified. JAMES BLACK

OPPOSITE: Polly King, a Niagara Falls artist, makes styles come to life on WBEN-TV in August 1951. Mrs. King sketched an original suit worn by model Jackie Coleman, center, as Allene Buckley admired the result. The models made several changes during shooting of the "Wonderland" fashion program, which was broadcast every Monday afternoon at 1:45 pm on WBEN-TV. BUFFALO NEWS ARCHIVES

ABOVE: Paul Hyde, assistant fire alarm dispatcher, checks alarms in May 1951. BUFFALO NEWS ARCHIVES

ABOVE RIGHT: Freighter "Penobscot" burns in the Buffalo Harbor in October 1951 after a collision with barge Morania loaded with 3,500,000 gallons of gasoline. BUFFALO NEWS ARCHIVES

RIGHT: Street cleaners Joseph Capalano and Thomas Dianno sweeping away the debris of winter at Main and Exchange streets in February 1951. BUFFALO NEWS ARCHIVES

OPPOSITE: Downtown Buffalo in the early 1950s. BUFFALO NEWS ARCHIVES

LEFT: With the lakes navigation season closing, ships are anchored "bumper to bumper" at some of Buffalo's winter berthing docks as seen in this December 1951 photograph of freighters in the City Ship Canal. BUFFALO NEWS ARCHIVES

OPPOSITE TOP LEFT: Couples at Town Casino celebrating Samuel Marino's last night before leaving for his service in the Navy in 1951. From left: Carol Della Penta, Anthony Perez, Marie Gigliotti, Jack Armitage, Samuel Marino, Frances DeCarlo. MARIE GIGLIOTTI

OPPOSITE BOTTOM LEFT: Canisius College Golden Griffins hockey team in 1951. George Wopperer is in the top row, fifth from right. MARCIA WOPPERER

OPPOSITE RIGHT: President Harry S. Truman and first lady Bess Truman stop in Buffalo to campaign for Democrats Anthony Tauriello and Chester Gorski on Oct. 9, 1952. The rally was held at Memorial Hall. BUFFALO NEWS ARCHIVES

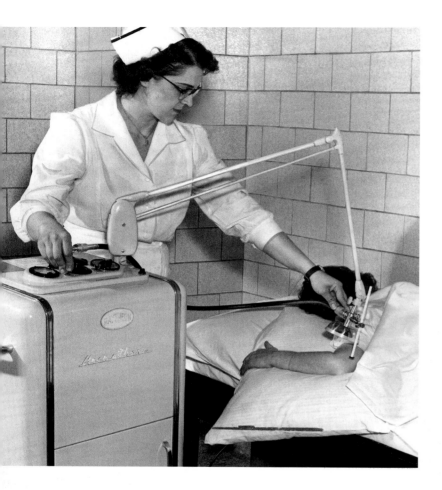

ABOVE: Miss Ida L. Anzideo, a physical therapist, adjusts Mercy Hospital's new microwave diathermy unit to give a patient a localized deep-heat treatment in March 1952. BUFFALO NEWS ARCHIVES

RIGHT: Buffalo teens do the Bunny Hop on Bob Wells' Hi-Teen show, circa 1952. BUFFALO NEWS ARCHIVES

OPPOSITE: A "water taxi" was pressed into service in Buffalo Harbor for the benefit of crews aboard lake ships idled by the steel strike and tied up at the breakwall in June 1952. A whistle or searching signal calls the sea-going taxi any time of the day or night. Elmer Claire and Edward Trombley of Frontier Marine Supply operated this "taxi." BUFFALO NEWS ARCHIVES

ABOVE: Gayle and Priscilla Less decked out in western outfits at the Buffalo Zoo in 1952. PRISCILLA KNISLEY

ABOVE LEFT: The biggest single job tackled by the American Ship Building Company, was the modernization of this freighter, the "E.A.S. Clarke", seen here in December 1952. BUFFALO NEWS ARCHIVES

LEFT: Yvonne Runfola on the sidewalk in front of a Costanzo's Bread truck on Porter Avenue in the early 1950s. DIANE E. RUNFOLA

OPPOSITE: Daniel S. Grandillo Sr. stands outside his store with his dog Trixie at 208 Main St., circa 1952. DANA KELLEY

ABOVE: Kensington High School senior class, 1952. CAROL PYTEL

RIGHT: Canisius College ROTC took part in the United Irish-American Association St. Patrick's Day Parade along Main Street in March 1953. Approximately 50,000 spectators watched the 25,000 marchers during the annual parade. BUFFALO NEWS ARCHIVES

OPPOSITE TOP LEFT: Buffalo Schoolmasters Association at Kudera's Grove in 1952. The association was formed in 1894 by some teachers, administrators, engineers and tradesmen of the Buffalo Public Schools. Primarily a social organization, the group held picnics and banquets and annually honors a member for being an outstanding schoolman. SCHOOLMASTERS ASSOCIATION/TOM BREEN

OPPOSITE BOTTOM LEFT: Members of a class, including people from 18 countries, gather around the globe in the International Institute and point to their original homelands in March 1953. They are, from left: Mrs. Victonn La Hood, Lebanon; Dominic Ferlan, Italy; Mrs. Elizabeth Goannada, France; Miss Maria Taksdal, Norway; George Manuschakow, Soviet Russia; Mun Fong Chin, China. BUFFALO NEWS ARCHIVES

OPPOSITE RIGHT: Margaret McDonald Hanratty and Owen P. Hanratty outside of St. Joseph's Cathedral on Franklin Street in 1952. MARGARET SIPENEK

ABOVE: City officials inspect new radar device that checks on speeders on June 25, 1953. "This radar scope will tell the police how fast a car is speeding," Wade Stevenson, chairman of the Board of Safety, left, tells Mayor Mruk, center, and Police Commissioner Noeppel. BUFFALO NEWS ARCHIVES

LEFT: A wire photo machine put into operation in the Buffalo Police Bureau of Investigation in October 1953 allowed the city to join 25 other American law-enforcement agencies that used machines of this kind to transmit photographs and fingerprints. At left is Henry J. Maxwell, assistant chief of the bureau. Police Photographer Albert Hauser tries out the machine. BUFFALO NEWS ARCHIVES

OPPOSITE: Niagara Frontier Transit operators Earl H. Griffin, Albert J. Thompson, Henry E. Prentice and Francis W. Sturm inspect a newly purchased bus in October 1953. It was purchased for $22,000 and included conventional leaf springs replaced by eight air bellows made of nylon tire fabric, supplemented by aircraft-type shock absorbers. BUFFALO NEWS ARCHIVES

ABOVE: Sister Eugene, administrator of Sisters' Hospital, tries out the controls on an instrument for making encephalographs, or x-ray photographs of the brain in December 1953. Watching are Mrs. J. Leo Scanlon, left, and Mrs. Robert K. Gillen of Louise de Marillac, the donor. BUFFALO NEWS ARCHIVES

RIGHT: South Buffalo native Cy Williams, far right, wishes a safe journey to Warner "Babe" Birrer, far left, at the Central Train Station, circa 1954. Birrer, who pitched for the Detroit Tigers, Baltimore Orioles and Los Angeles Dodgers from 1955-1958, graduated from Kensington High School in 1947. He was signed by Williams, a longtime scout for the Tigers. ED WILLIAMS

OPPOSITE: A Coast Guard cutter assists in fighting a blaze at the foot of Michigan Street on Sept. 21, 1953. BUFFALO NEWS ARCHIVES

LEFT: Installing a traffic light as part of the newly installed synchronized system are Eugene R. Corrigan, left, and John J. Hanehan in March 1954. BUFFALO NEWS ARCHIVES

OPPOSITE TOP LEFT: Firemen search the ruins of the Cleveland Hill Elementary School Annex where 10 pupils died and 28 were injured in a tragic fire on March 31, 1954. BUFFALO NEWS ARCHIVES

OPPOSITE BOTTOM LEFT: Dr. Herman E. Hilleboe, left, and Gov. Thomas Dewey look over the smoking machine for mice at the Roswell Park Institute dedication on Oct. 14, 1954. BUFFALO NEWS ARCHIVES

OPPOSITE TOP RIGHT: The Buffalo Skyway nears completion in November 1954. BUFFALO NEWS ARCHIVES

OPPOSITE BOTTOM RIGHT: Keys to the sleek new Sister Kenny Ambulance for Polio Victims was a gift from the Buffalo Federation of Labor, December 1953. AFL Leader Clayton F. Stephenson, at wheel, presents keys to Alan K. Sawyer, local Sister Kenny Foundation president; while BFL President Charles W. Halloran and Foundation Managing Director James A. Gilbert, right, look on. Sister Elizabeth Kenny was an Australian nurse who as early as 1910 had reported treating polio cases in the bush back "to normalcy." She came to the United States to Minneapolis (Medical School of the University of Minnesota) in 1940. While many were skeptical of her ideas, she was met with immediate support at the Medical School of the University of Minnesota. In 1952, shortly after her death, the Sister Kenny Foundation was formed by supporters. BUFFALO NEWS ARCHIVES

ABOVE: Bishop Timon's senior prom at the Glen Casino in Williamsville in June 1954. At bottom left are John "Jack" Heitzhaus and Patricia Volkennerm, who would be married July 28, 1956. MARY HEITZHAUS LOMBARDO

RIGHT: Linda Doucet (center) and friends on West Avenue, circa 1954. LINDA DOUCET

OPPOSITE: This turbo-supercharged engine, capable of ratings up to 5,000 horsepower, was being made at Worthington's Buffalo works for a western power plant in October 1955. BUFFALO NEWS ARCHIVES

ABOVE: Richard Miller, age 10, heads the line as children of St. Mary of Sorrow School's first four grades line up to receive their first Salk anti-polio immunization shots from Dr. W.C. Byrnes on May 18, 1955. BUFFALO NEWS ARCHIVES

ABOVE LEFT: Health Commissioner Edward B. Bukowski loads his car with the shipment of Salk Polio vaccine flown into Buffalo by American Airlines in 1955. The vaccine was given to children in the first four grades of Buffalo schools. BUFFALO NEWS ARCHIVES

LEFT: Attacking at several points, firefighters bring under control a blaze that heavily damaged St. John Kanty's Church shortly after it broke out on Jan. 13, 1955. The fire started in the altar on the right side of the main sanctuary. Heat burst 10 stained-glass windows. BUFFALO NEWS ARCHIVES

OPPOSITE: Aerial view of Buffalo, circa 1955. BUFFALO NEWS ARCHIVES

ABOVE: The Buffalo Skyway, the city's new high-level bridge, came under scrutiny as state and city officials made an inspection trip over the new structure on Oct. 4, 1955. Standing on the east side of the bridge, overlooking Main Street, are, from left: George F. Collins, acting city traffic adviser; Walter M. Maday, Board of Safety member; Charles T. Love, city engineer; Mayor Pankow. The Skyway opened to traffic later in the month. BUFFALO NEWS ARCHIVES

ABOVE RIGHT: Singer Tony Bennett, second from left, at a table with Connie Colangelo, left, and her friends Frank and Sarah Vaccaro, in the Town Casino, circa 1955. DOMINIC COLANGELO

RIGHT: Five Fiore siblings and their spouses share a drink at the Town Casino, circa 1955. From left: Jim Amone, Ed Penders, Tom Fiore, Lu (Phinney) Fiore, Mary (Alex) Fiore, Paul Fiore, Esther (Kogut) Fiore, Frank Fiore, Mary (Fiore) Penders, Eleanor (Fiore) Amone. CRAIG PENDERS/PEGGY PENDERS TRONDONE

OPPOSITE: A view of traffic at Niagara Square from City Hall in July 1955. BUFFALO NEWS ARCHIVES

ABOVE: Fifth-grade class at School 62 in 1955. BILL BITTERMAN

OPPOSITE TOP LEFT: Annual motorcycle blessing at St. Christopher's Church in 1955. At left are siblings Arlene M. Shulz and Paul R. Shulz. Paul's Harley Davidson is being blessed. ARLENE NEELY

OPPOSITE BOTTOM LEFT: The Most Rev. Joseph A. Burke, bishop of Buffalo from 1952 to 1962, awarding the "Jewel of Honor" to Major Charles E. Shulz Sr., Knights of St. John, Commandery 292 of St. Mary of Sorrow Church in 1955. ARLENE NEELY

OPPOSITE TOP RIGHT: Karima Bondi with her father, John, at 238 Seventh St., circa 1955. KARIMA BONDI

OPPOSITE BOTTOM RIGHT: Rosalyn M. Kick and Albert J. Maggioli preparing to attend St. Joseph Collegiate Institute's senior prom in 1955. The couple would marry in 1960 and raise five children: Mark, Kevin, Maria, Lisa, Michelle. Their five children gave them 13 grandchildren. A. MAGGIOLI

ABOVE: Holiday gathering of the Vincent Gazzo family on Elmwood Avenue in 1956. From left: Vincent Gazzo, Len Testa, Rose Testa, Agnes Gazzo, Mary Gazzo. LEONARD A. TESTA

ABOVE RIGHT: The New York Central's new Aerotrain, an experimental, light-weight "dream train" built by General Motors made an appearance in Buffalo in 1956. BUFFALO NEWS ARCHIVES

RIGHT: The Fire Department took over the Engine 20 building, home base of the city fireboat "Edward M. Cotter" in June 1956. BUFFALO NEWS ARCHIVES

OPPOSITE: These youths were arrested when police stopped their car and relieved them of an arsenal of clubs, knives and razors on June 1, 1956. Police stopped their car for a routine check after being alerted for trouble at the Lakeview Housing Project. The rise of gangs and hoodlums presented a significant challenge for Buffalo authorities in the 1950s. Delinquency rates in Buffalo in the mid-1950s were substantially higher than in New York City. BUFFALO NEWS ARCHIVES

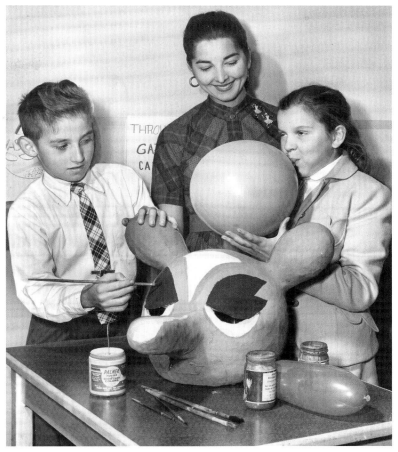

ABOVE: Students at School 78, on Olympic Avenue, are busy preparing for Halloween in 1956. James R. Ahrens, age 10, and Carol L. Phelps, age 11, are making papier-mache Halloween masks under the supervision of art instructor Mrs. Adam A. Malik. BUFFALO NEWS ARCHIVES

LEFT: The German Catholic Orphan Home after a portion of the main section burned in January 1956. BUFFALO NEWS ARCHIVES

OPPOSITE: The Right Rev. Msgr. Roman J. Nuwer helps the children of the German Catholic Orphan Home board a bus after the orphanage burned. BUFFALO NEWS ARCHIVES

ABOVE: Robert Robertson, a member of the 65 Club on the Towpath, tosses a rocking chair as club members prepare to make way for the new Niagara Thruway (I-190) on April 1, 1957. Other members are preparing to move their boat to another site along the Niagara River. BUFFALO NEWS ARCHIVES

ABOVE RIGHT: Charles J. Campbell, right, handing car keys to a customer at Mernan Chevrolet, 2751 Bailey Ave., circa 1956. Campbell was the first African-American car salesman at Mernan Chevrolet. The dealership closed in 1993 after nearly 50 years of operation. CHARLES H. CAMPBELL

RIGHT: A sixth-grade class at School 72 in November 1956. The school was located at 71 Lorraine Ave. Joseph Rauls is in the row of standing students, second from the left. KIRK AND PEGGY KLEIN

OPPOSITE: Downtown Buffalo in the 1950s. BUFFALO NEWS ARCHIVES

ABOVE: Delaware Park with Lincoln Parkway bridge at right in 1957. This view is looking toward the David statue from the top of old Elmwood Bridge. JOHN GOODMAN

ABOVE LEFT: Grace DeGraff Hoffman, left, and Marcia Grace Hoffman Machemer on the bumper of the family's new 1957 Buick in Amherst in the summer of 1957. KAREN HOFFMAN MCKE

LEFT: A visit to Santa at Sattler's Department Store at 998 Broadway, circa 1957. From left: Vincent Marlowe, Elizabeth Marlowe and Marlene Marlowe Campanella. MARLENE CAMPANELLA

OPPOSITE: The workers with the finest view of Buffalo in October 1957 were these men who were doing the $400,000 job of repairing the 398-foot tower roof on City Hall. From left are George F. Hess, Edward J. Peters, Harold W. Seifert and August Aumer. BUFFALO NEWS ARCHIVES

ABOVE: Miss Tosca Biscaro demonstrates low-level steps on one of the newly purchased buses by Niagara Frontier Transit Company in December 1958. BUFFALO NEWS ARCHIVES

ABOVE RIGHT: Five patrolmen join the motorcycle squad in March 1958. From left: Francis J. Deacon, Francis L. Conroy, Louis N. Pelonero, Raymond P. Berni, Frederick A. Shumacher. BUFFALO NEWS ARCHIVES

RIGHT: Soccer team at Delaware Park consisting of refugees from the 1956 Hungarian Revolution. MARY NEMETH

OPPOSITE: First-year tap dance class at Rogers Studio above a movie theater on Grant Street, circa 1957. Pamela Meyer is seated at right. PAMELA SNYDER

LEFT: Firefighters aboard the "Edward M. Cotter" pour water on a large concrete storage bin at General Mills Inc., 54 Michigan St., in an effort to prevent flames from spreading to adjacent bins as they battle a stubborn wheat fire in August 1958. BUFFALO NEWS ARCHIVES

OPPOSITE TOP: Central Park Shopping Plaza in April 1958. BUFFALO NEWS ARCHIVES

OPPOSITE BOTTOM: Rising steel continued to change the complexion of lower Main Street in October 1958. This view includes the old Michigan Avenue bridge in the foreground and was taken from the top of the Fairmont Creamery Building. BUFFALO NEWS ARCHIVES

ABOVE: Szuder's Dry Cleaners and Friendly Inn Tavern on the corner of South Park Avenue and Alabama Street, circa 1958. Owners Bruno and Emily Szuder operated the cleaners from 1945 to 1963. DENNIS SZUDER & CAROLANNE SZUDER KERL

RIGHT: A 1932 Ford Roadster hot rod at the 1958 Clutch Artists Auto-Rama at Buffalo Memorial Auditorium. CLUTCH ARTISTS OF BUFFALO

OPPOSITE: Chef Felix pizza truck at the Erie County Fair, August 1958. Established in 1957, Chef Felix Pizzeria on Wheels was the first food truck in Western New York. Felix P. Coniglio came up with the idea when he was a baker on the USS "Boston" during World War II. He made pizza for his shipmates and they loved it. He then said to himself, "How can I make pizza and bring it to customers freshly baked when I get out of the Navy?" That's when it came to him, a mobile unit, a truck. FELIX J. CONIGLIO

ABOVE: The three-wheel mailster was introduced into the Buffalo Post Office in 1959. This vehicle could carry 500 pounds of mail while the foot carrier was limited to 35 pounds of mail. BUFFALO NEWS ARCHIVES

LEFT: Miss Nancy A. Miller, 18, of 277 Bissell Ave., demonstrates Roswell Park Memorial Institute's fractionating device in February 1959. Used in studies of the possible relation between cigarette smoking and cancer, the device separates tobacco tars. BUFFALO NEWS ARCHIVES

OPPOSITE: Steelworkers make themselves comfortable on the picket line during the long strike in October 1959. Along with food, drinks and a canvas shelter, on World Series days, a television was set up using company power. Picketing Bethlehem Steel's Lackawanna plant are members of Local 261, United Steelworkers of America. BUFFALO NEWS ARCHIVES

ABOVE: Danny Allman, age 6, Tennessee Street in the "Old First Ward," circa 1959. DANIEL ALLMAN

ABOVE RIGHT: Crystal Beach in July 1959. BUFFALO NEWS ARCHIVES

RIGHT: Emergency Hospital – a haven of care for the city's sick and injured for 75 years – announced it was closing its doors in 1959. The announcement blamed the financial squeeze and a shortage of nursing and technical personnel. BUFFALO NEWS ARCHIVES

OPPOSITE: An aerial view of downtown Buffalo in November 1959. BUFFALO NEWS ARCHIVES

ABOVE: Original members of Clutch Artists, circa 1959. The club was founded in 1954. Front row, from left: Rolland Brennan, Paul Kaufman, Joe Rusz, Ron Smith, Greg Gibson, John Watson, Don Moreno. Back row: Ken Gill, Marty Brennan, Dan Cutin, Skip Kazmark. CLUTCH ARTISTS OF BUFFALO

LEFT: David and Doris Orr walking down the aisle after getting married in April 1959. DORIS ORR

OPPOSITE: Softball team sponsored by the Blan-Mar Cocktail Lounge at 178 Chester St. in the Cold Springs area of Buffalo. Standing in front of the team are Proprietors Blanchet Turner, left, and Marion Jackson. The business was in operation from 1955 to 1963. CHARLES H. CAMPBELL

INDEX

Looking for more Buffalo history?

Buffalo Memories II

THE EARLY YEARS AND THE 1940s

Excerpts and photos taken from
*"Well Done – From Skipping Class to First Class.
The Life and Times of Russell J. Salvatore"*,
written by Joseph Giambra.

Russell J. Salvatore

Russell Salvatore says his mother and father were the strictest parents in the world. But, he and his siblings, Mary and Tony, loved their parents unconditionally in spite of their sternness.

Joseph Salvatore may have been a strict father but everyone in the neighborhood loved him for his extreme generosity, a trait that Russell obviously inherited. During the Great Depression, Joe Salvatore fed the neighborhood. He owned the space on East Delavan Avenue that ultimately became Salvatore's Restaurant. But at that time, it was a grocery store. In back of the store was the Salvatore speakeasy. The bushels of bananas, apples, oranges and vegetables that Joe Salvatore dispensed freely to the hungry during Prohibition, were both a Godsend to the poor, and a successful front for illegal booze.

Photos provided by Donna Stewart

Joe Salvatore insisted his children take music lessons. Mary studied piano, Tony the banjo, and Russell studied guitar with the great Tony Militello. During World War II, on Easter Sunday, April 25, 1943, Russell and Anthony went to radio station WEBR on North Street to sing and play Irving Berlin's Easter Parade on Uncle Bill's Children's Hour. The winner of this amateur show was determined by the amount of letters and penny postcards the radio station received on behalf of a contestant.

First prize was a 25 dollar War Bond. Second prize was a pair of 'high tops' from Liberty Shoes. By Wednesday of the following week, WEBR announced that The Singing Salvatores not only won, but they broke the record for most votes ever received in Uncle Bill's lengthy history. So enormous was the amount, WEBR presented The Singing Salvatores with two 25 dollar War Bonds, and two pairs of high tops.

As a youth, Russell Salvatore had no fondness for the restaurant business. He was going to high school. "I'm naturally from Italian descent", he says "and by being Italian, you know, you always had to pay attention to your older brother. In the '50s, when my brother, Tony -- who was three years older than me -- was drafted, I left high school to help my father run the corner saloon on East Delavan. . Well, that was the start of my falling in love with this business. I ran the place, and the rest is history.

russell's
STEAKS · CHOPS · & MORE

Russell looks back fondly on his days serving in the US Army, despite missing the birth of his first born child, his beautiful daughter Rosemarie. As a result, across from his Grand Hotel, Russell Salvatore has dedicated his Patriots and Heroes Park to immortalize fallen veterans, first responders, and all those who perished on 9-11 and in the ill-fated flight 3407 on February 12, 2009. Patriots and Heroes Park is a gesture of love and appreciation from Russell Salvatore to the grieving families, and a gift to his beloved community. "The park is for people to enjoy and to reflect. I want them to know it will always be there, complete with a 30x60' American flag flying above it."

J. SALVATORE'S
RESTAURANT

Russell J. Salvatore's
Patriots & Heroes Park

photos by
donna stewart

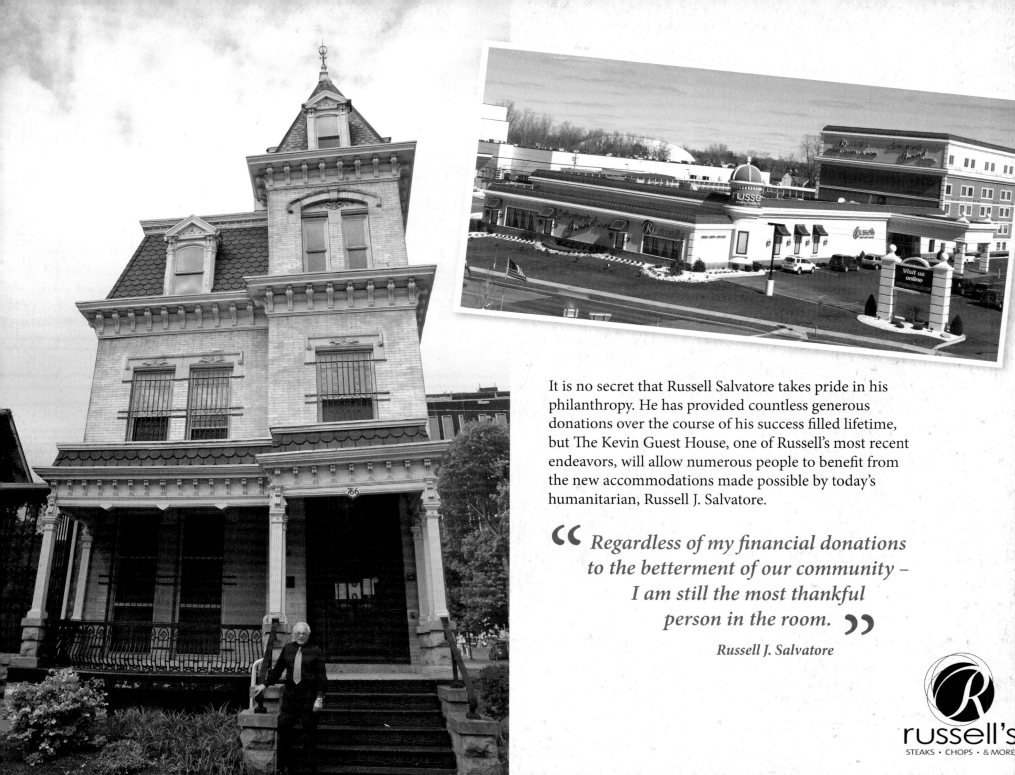

It is no secret that Russell Salvatore takes pride in his philanthropy. He has provided countless generous donations over the course of his success filled lifetime, but The Kevin Guest House, one of Russell's most recent endeavors, will allow numerous people to benefit from the new accommodations made possible by today's humanitarian, Russell J. Salvatore.

" *Regardless of my financial donations to the betterment of our community – I am still the most thankful person in the room.* **"**

Russell J. Salvatore

russell's
STEAKS · CHOPS · & MORE

Looking for more Buffalo history?

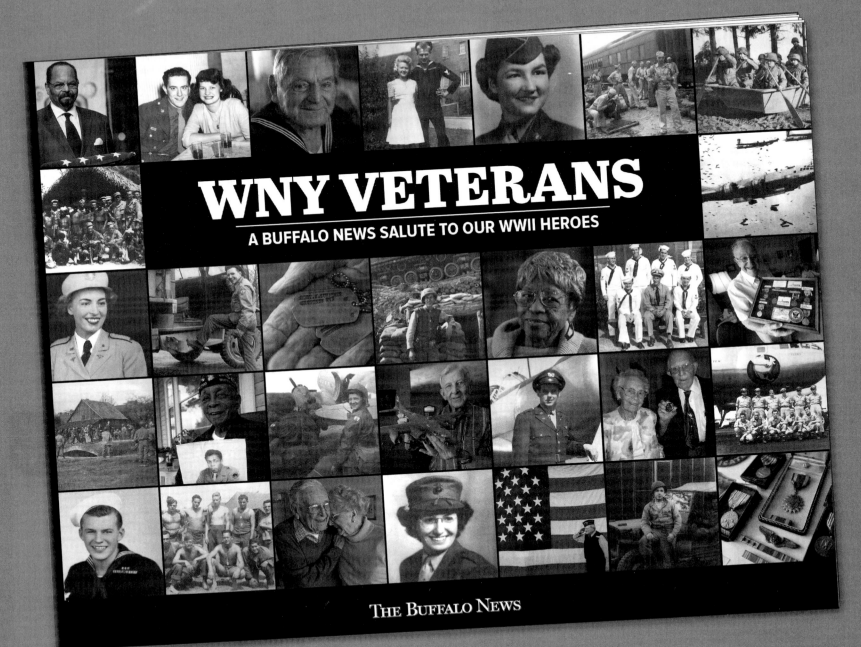

WNY VETERANS

A BUFFALO NEWS SALUTE TO OUR WWII HEROES

THE BUFFALO NEWS

Looking for more Buffalo history?

The Blizzard of '77

Buffalo's Storm of the Century